Wheels

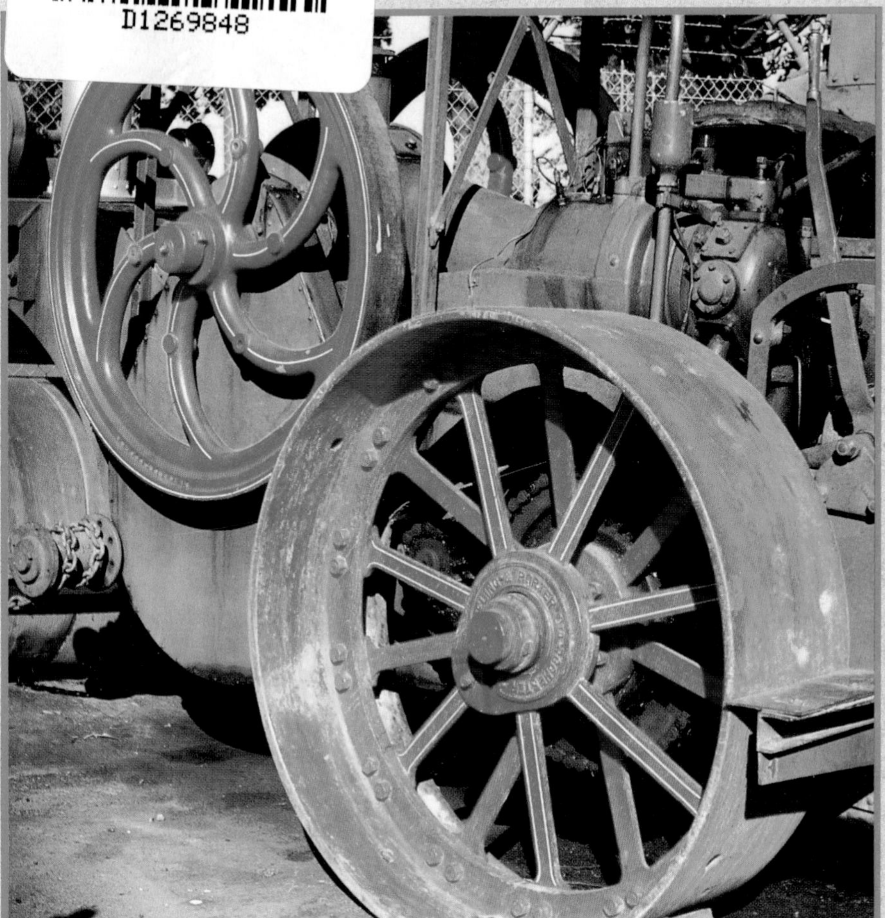

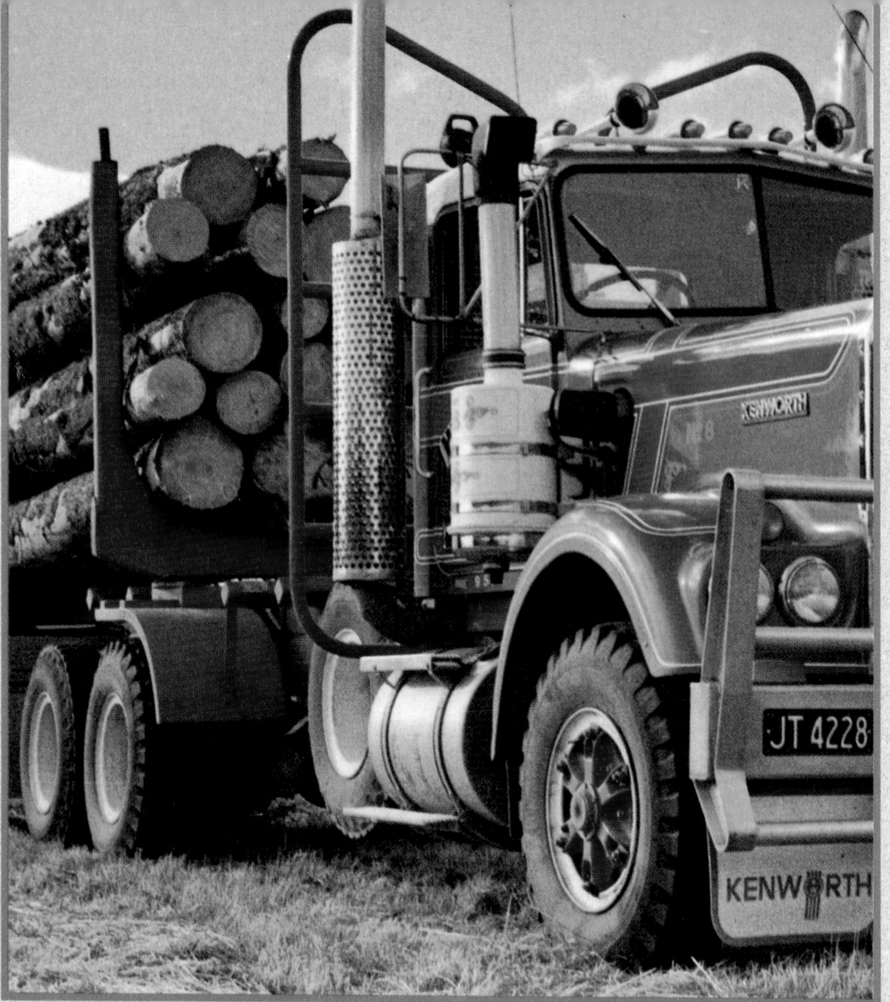

Wheels on trucks,

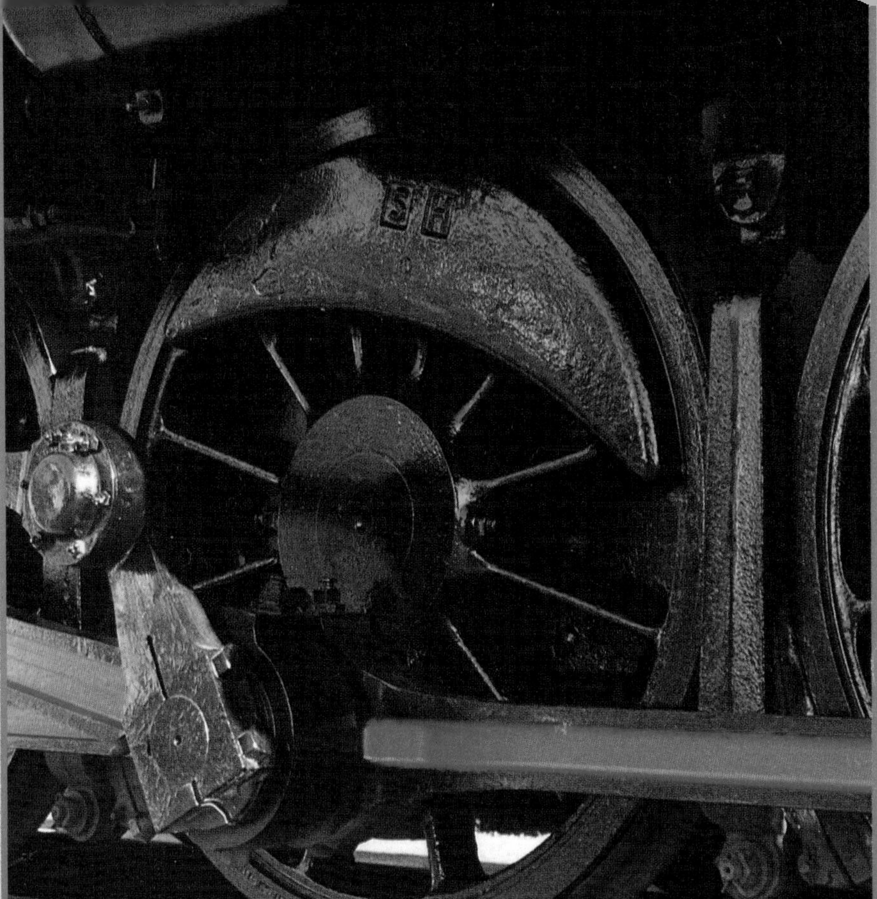

wheels on trains,

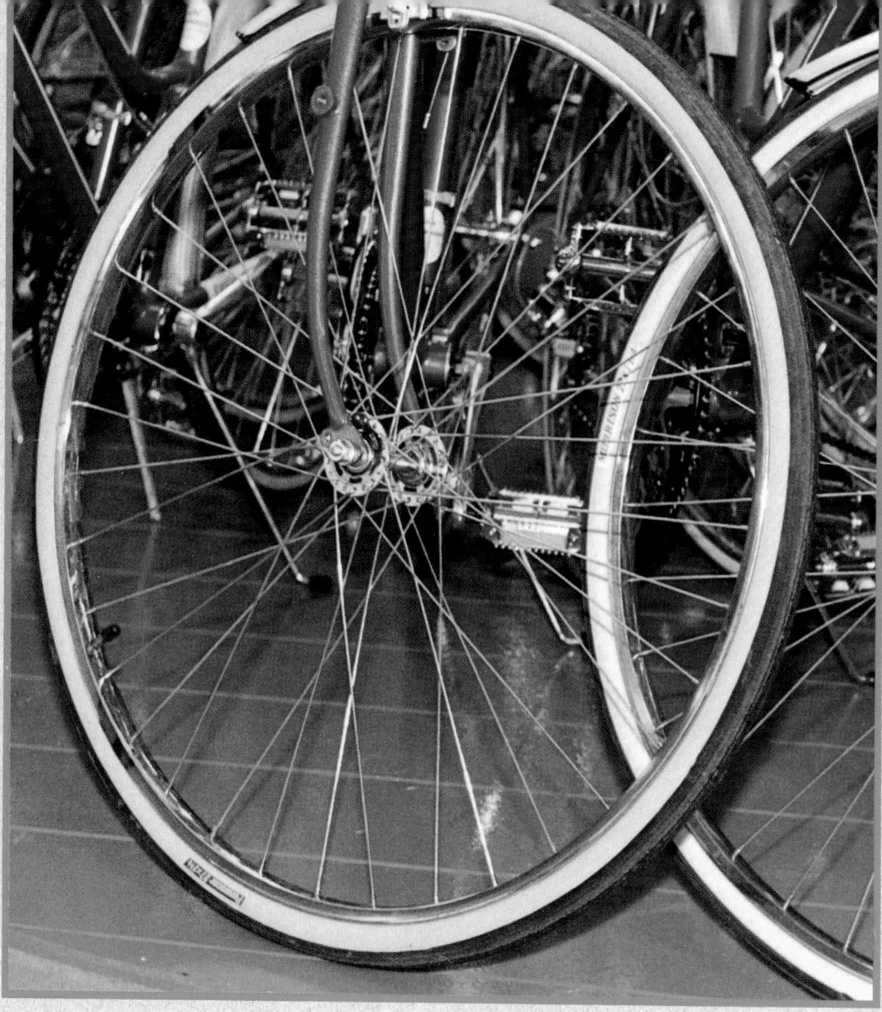

wheels on bikes,

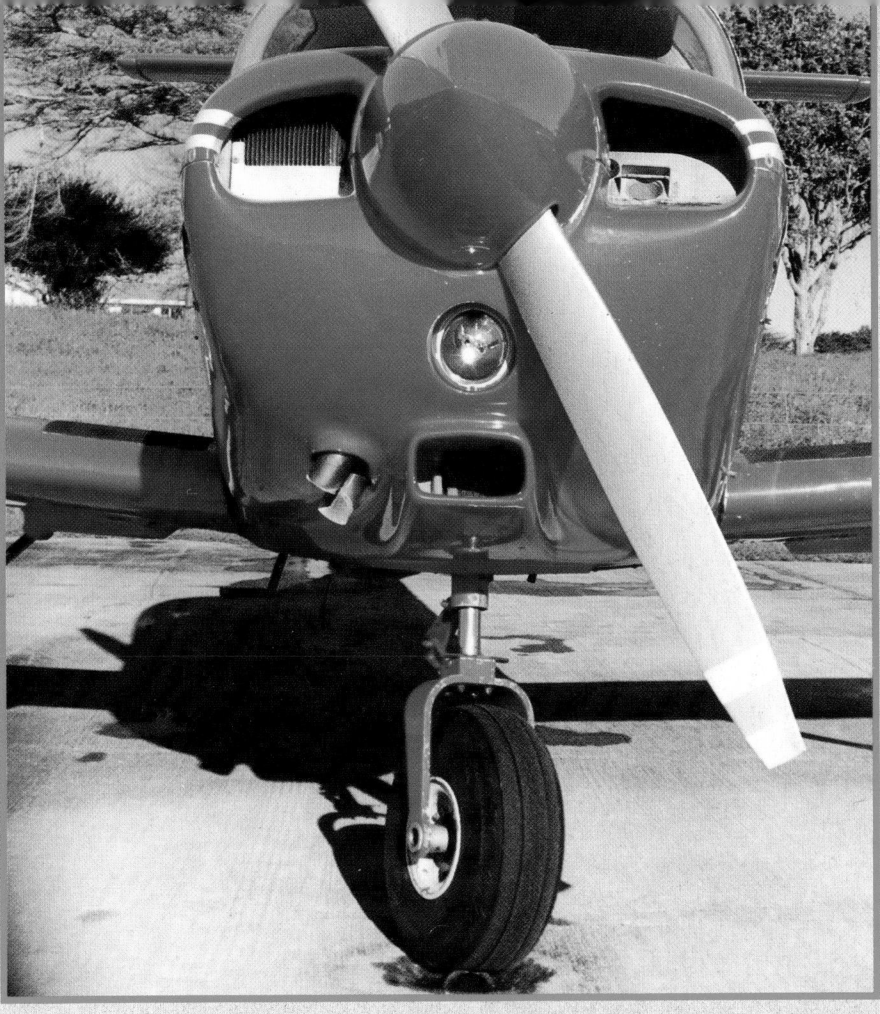

wheels on planes,

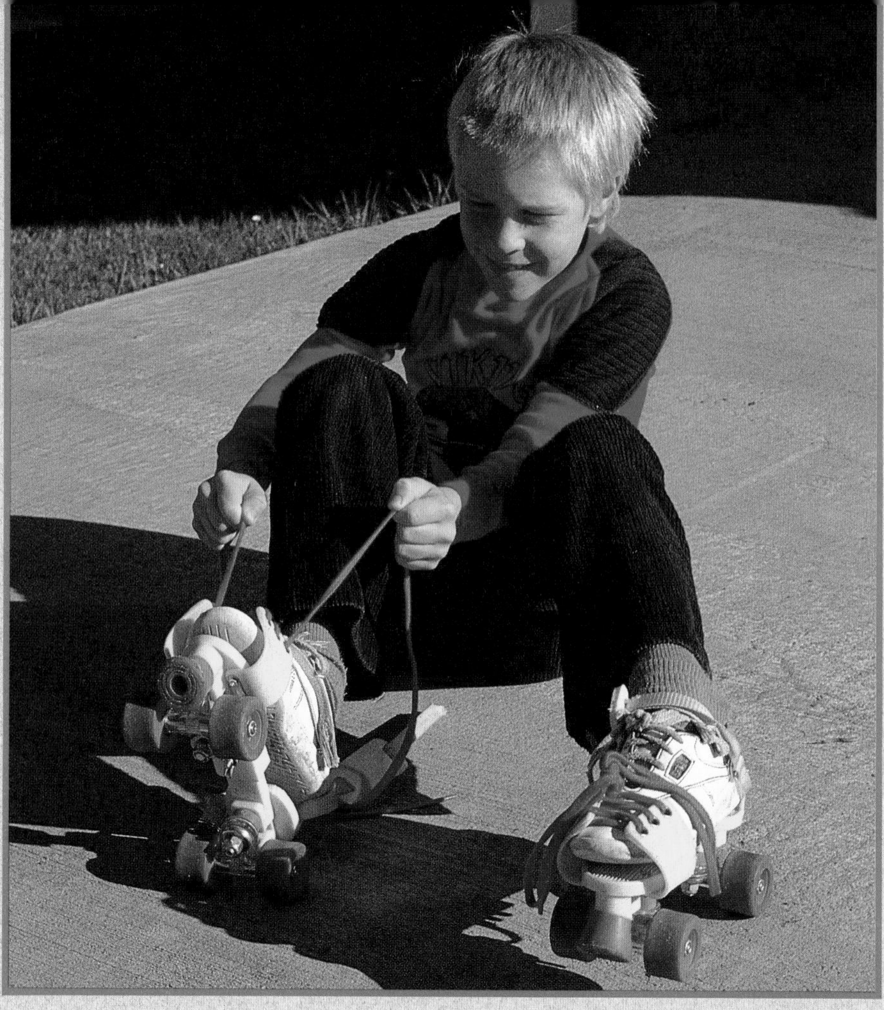

wheels on skates,

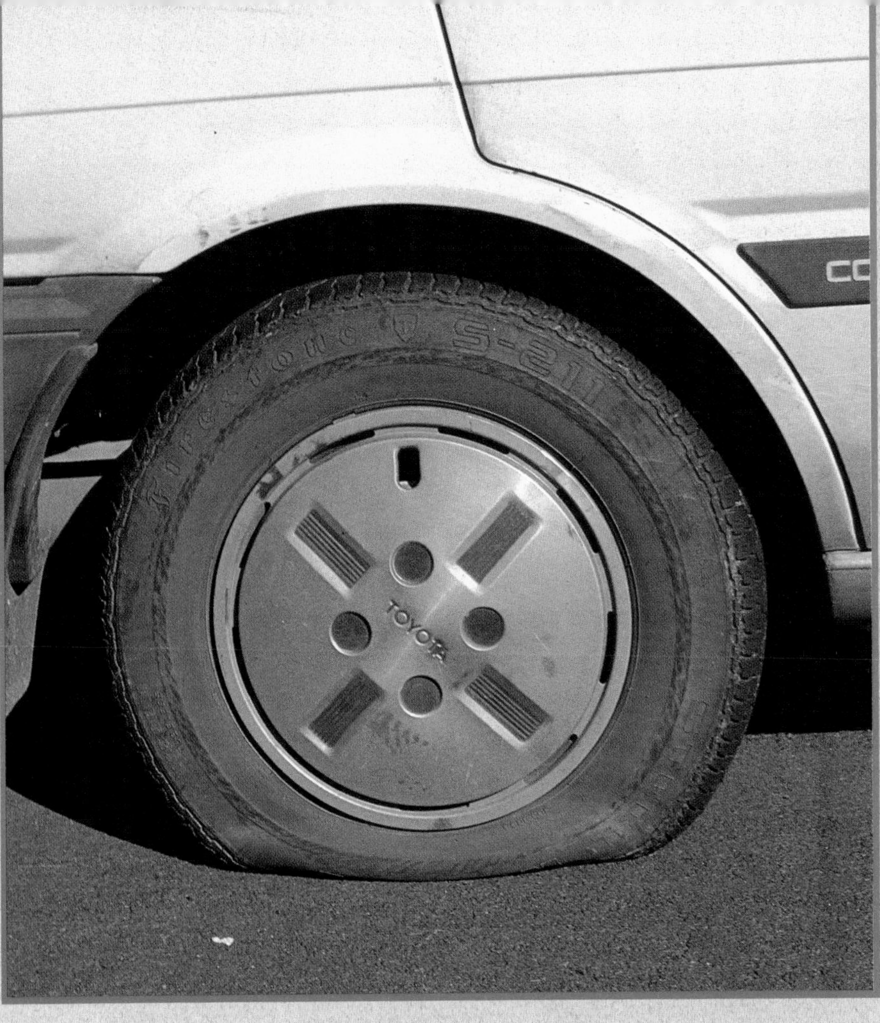

wheels on the ground —

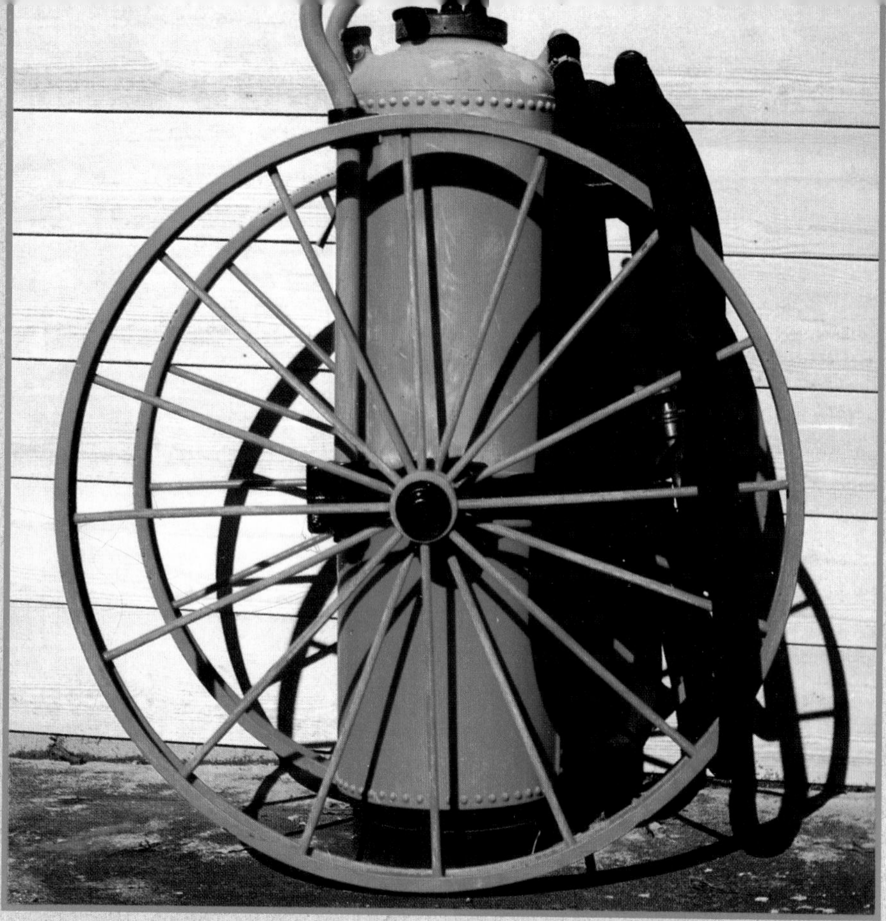

all kinds of wheels
go round and round.